IONIZING INNOVATION: UNRAVELING THE PRINCIPLES OF LITHIUM-ION CELLS VOL.1

How does a lithium cell work? Demystifying Lithium-Ion Cells and Their Core Technological Principles

May 2023 edition

DISCLAIMER: This publication aims to elucidate core principles of battery technology and is anticipated to evolve in tandem with the progression of the field. The focus herein is primarily on fostering a comprehensive understanding rather than exact precision. While every effort has been made to ensure the accuracy and reliability of the information presented, the author does not assume liability for any inaccuracies or their repercussions. Feedback, corrections, and suggestions for enhancements are greatly appreciated and can be communicated directly via email. Please be aware that reliance on the information contained within this document is at the reader's discretion.

Oriol Gallemí Rovira, PhD-Eng.

ChatGPT 4.0 – assisted draft

oriol@electrificat.com

First mention to my family, Alex, Max and Mag. I love you so much and you let me write this in my scarce time at home. This is your gift to me.

To all my mentors, professors, customers, suppliers and colleagues, from which I learnt everything I know today.

Table of contents

Lithium-based cell working principle 2
    A controlled chain reaction. 3
    A small step for an ion, a giant leap for the cell 4
    Half and half reactions. A full potential 4
    Construction: a laminated approach 7
    Binders: a scaffold for better performance 8
Cathode: the natural attractor 9
    The role of Nickel in cathode 12
    The role of Manganese in cathode 12
    The role of Cobalt in cathode 13
    The role of Aluminum in cathode 13
    The role of Phosphate (PO_4) in cathode 14
    The role of Sulfur in cathode 15
    The role of Yttrium in LFP cathode 16
Anode, the holder 16
    The role of Graphite in anode 17
    The role of Hard Carbon in anode 19
    The role of Silicon in anode 20
    The role of LTO in anode 20
Generating voltage 21
Making a cell alive 23
    Formation 23
    The SEI, a live component of the cell 25
    The electrolyte: a conductive salt and solvent mix 27
    The separator: a must-have unpolluted 30
    Flame retardants: the key to keep safe redox running 31
Using a live cell 32
    C-rate takes it all 32

Internal reactions absorb and release electrical, mechanical and thermal energy 32
Temperature sensitivity 33
Lithium plating 33
Battery venting...34
A long-lasting life: cyclability..34
An always ready cell is a risk 35
Capacity fade, power decrease and voltage drop: inefficiency...36
Charge: risk in the short run...36
Discharge: risks in the long run 37

Lithium-based cell working principle

Lithium-based cells also known as lithium-ion batteries, are a type of rechargeable (secondary) batteries that use lithium ions as charge carriers. They have many advantages over other types of batteries, such as higher energy density, longer lifespan, lower self-discharge rate, and no memory effect. However, they also have some drawbacks, such as high cost, safety issues, environmental impact, and limited availability of lithium.

There are different types of lithium-based batteries with different chemistries and performance characteristics. Some common examples are lithium iron phosphate (LFP), lithium cobalt oxide (LCO), lithium manganese oxide (LMO), and lithium nickel manganese cobalt oxide (NMC). They have been commonly used in a wide range of electronic devices such as appliances, industrial equipment, and electric vehicles since 1993.

The basic working principle of a lithium-ion battery involves the movement of lithium ions between the positive and negative electrodes of the battery. Lithium ions (very alkaline) which are forced to be sandwiched in the anode jump back to the ceramic, (strongly acidic) cathodes to restore a lower energy state.

The potential range is the voltage window that the electrodes operate in. The anode has a lower potential than the cathode, which means it releases electrons during discharge and accepts electrons during charge. The cathode has a higher potential than the anode, which means it accepts electrons during discharge and releases electrons during charge. The difference between their potentials determines the cell voltage. The point where both potentials match results in 0V at cell level, but they may also even revert under abuse.

When the battery is charged, lithium ions are extracted from the positive electrode, which is typically made of a lithium metal oxide mixture and move through a separator to the negative electrode, which is a few 50 microns away.

During discharge, the lithium ions move back through the separator from the negative electrode to the positive electrode, producing an electrical current that can power a device.

To recharge a lithium-ion battery, a voltage is applied to the battery in the opposite direction to the discharge process, causing the lithium ions to move back from the negative electrode to the positive electrode.

The movement of lithium ions is facilitated by the presence of an electrolyte, which is typically a lithium salt dissolved in an organic solvent. The electrolyte allows the lithium ions to flow freely between the electrodes, while the separator prevents the flow of electrons, which would result in a short circuit.

Lithium-ion batteries are popular due to their high energy density, long cycle life, and low self-discharge rate when compared with previous rechargeable cells such as Lead-acid, NiCd or NiMH. However, they do require careful handling and are sensitive to high temperatures, which can cause thermal runaway and even fires.

A controlled chain reaction.

During the charging of a lithium-ion cell, the following electrochemical phenomena occur:

1. An external electromotive force removes some electrons from the cathode, generating a potential gap on the anode side.
2. An electric field is generated within the electrode collectors, polarizing the various materials in between.
3. Lithium ions are repelled from the ceramic crystal structures, requiring some effort (overpotential).
4. The polar solvent orients itself in the field direction and begins its movement towards releasing the bulk lithium ions to the separator.
5. There is a loss due to viscosity, reflected as internal resistance, as moving such a large carrier is not straightforward.
6. To effectively release the Lithium ion, an overpotential is required. This adds to the transport loss.
7. The ion must pass the separator, which consumes a bit of energy to cover the gap.
8. Next, the ion must adhere again to another electrolyte transport carrier and be released at the solid electrolyte interphase (SEI) of a grain.
9. The thicker the graphite coating, the more difficult it is for the ion to reach the bottom grains near the electrode collector surface, as the ion has to pass through a labyrinth of touching particles, binders, and some contaminants.
10. The ion then has to dilute into the SEI and get intercalated inside the graphite laminates, pushing the interplanar distance a bit and meeting the missing electron. This step also consumes some additional overpotential.
11. As the process is not synchronous, the faster the charge is, the higher the concentration gradients and the overvoltages. This is similar to how a subway coach works, where not all particles go to their assigned seat straightforwardly and in a rush hour (fast charge), they need more pressure (overvoltage) to fit in the allocations.

12. This stress causes some degradation as it may trigger side reactions, with some molecules picking the other's atoms. This is similar to wallets in a subway's rush hour.

When the cell is stored, there is no electric field induced, and the electrolyte polarization is null. The charged anode is pushing the ions to leave the grains, but the non-ionized lithium atoms are not attracted by the charge carriers. The ones which are already bound do not find any incentive to leave the electrolyte and there is no potential gap among the two sides of the separator to push anything from one side to another. It is in equilibrium. Self-discharge mechanisms will be discussed further in advance.

The discharge happens in a similar fashion. Once an electric circuit is closed, the electrons escape thanks to the conductive graphite grains and additives and jump back to the cathode via the external wiring. An electric field is induced then between both plates. The electrolyte is polarized. The solid electrolyte interphase (SEI) experiences some gradient charging. Lithium ions are not comfortably set inside the graphite structure and feel somewhat pushed to go. And they go.

A small step for an ion, a giant leap for the cell

An advantage or disadvantage of closed cells is that the mass and center of gravity remains almost constant. Mass has a non-measurable variation and the center of gravity or inertia is just displaced a few 50 microns.

The lithium content of the battery is not given by the battery capacity alone. The lithium content is the amount of lithium metal or lithium ions that are present in the battery's active material. The active material is a powder mixture of the cathode and anode material (graphite, carbon), separator and electrolyte (organic solvent with dissolved lithium salts) usually with a particle size 0.8–0.1 mm.

To find out how much active lithium is in the battery, an estimation on how much energy each gram of lithium can store is required. This depends on various factors such as the type of cathode and anode material, their composition and structure, their electrolyte and SEI composition, their voltage range and efficiency, etc. One kilogram of lithium metal can store about 13.86 kWh of energy at standard conditions. However, this does not account for losses due to internal resistance, heat generation, self-discharge, etc. For reference, an old automotive 1865 NCA cathode 3250 mAh battery has a lithium content of about 0.0714 kg/kWh. This means that a 100 kWh battery would contain at least 7.14 kg of active lithium.

Put in perspective, an actual vehicle is moving 300 miles thanks to roughly 10 kg of lithium jumping a half of a human hair thick gap.

Half and half reactions. A full potential

A functional cell in a battery is constructed with two primary components: the anode and the cathode. These two elements form the backbone of the battery's operation, with each playing a distinct role in the energy transfer process. The anode holds a lower potential than the cathode during operation, and the difference between the electrode coating materials determines the net open circuit voltage of the battery.

While this description may seem straightforward, the reality is that not all material pairs function in the same way. They differ in several aspects, including how they transfer charge, how they host, hold, and release the carriers, and the different energy bands used for these processes. These variations contribute to a wide spectrum of efficiencies and energy content in different types of batteries.

The anode and cathode are coated with different materials, each chosen for their specific properties. For instance, in a lithium-ion battery, the anode is typically coated with graphite, a material that can intercalate lithium ions between its layers. The cathode, on the other hand, is often coated with a lithium metal oxide, which can also intercalate lithium ions but at a higher voltage. The choice of these materials is crucial as it determines the battery's voltage, capacity, and overall performance.

Different materials have different ways of hosting, holding, and releasing charge carriers. For example, some materials can intercalate a large number of lithium ions, providing a high capacity, while others can intercalate ions at a higher voltage, providing a higher energy content. Some materials can release and accept ions quickly, enabling high power output, while others can hold onto ions tightly, providing a long cycle life.

The energy bands used for these processes also vary between materials. In a material, the energy band refers to the range of energy levels that electrons can have. The valence band is filled with electrons, while the conduction band is typically empty. When an electron gains enough energy to jump from the valence band to the conduction band, it can move freely and contribute to electrical conductivity. The energy required to make this jump, known as the bandgap, varies between materials and affects their electrical properties.

In a battery, the energy bands of the electrode materials play a crucial role. When a lithium ion is intercalated into an electrode material, an electron is also added to balance the charge. This electron goes into the conduction band of the material, and the energy level of this band influences the voltage of the battery. Materials with a higher conduction band provide a higher voltage.

To validate the materials, scientists perform experiments in half-cell format. This is to split anode and cathode and explore each one response to current flow. Therefore just a few materials hold the matching capabilities of reversibility, stability, toxicity, abundance, manufacturability and cost effectiveness required on commercial, reliable, long-lasting products.

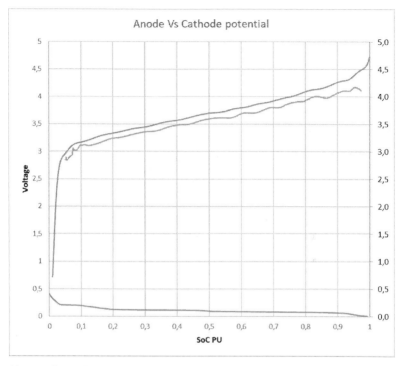

The top figure displays an oversized sample Graphite Anode (blue line) Vs a NMC Cathode (orange line). The cell OCV is displayed in grey, representing the theoretical measurable voltage. At its 0 SoC, Anode and Cathode potentials are the same, while at 100% differ at its maximum.

As an illustrative example, lithium (Li) possesses an extraordinarily low standard potential of -3.04 V vs Standard Hydrogen Electrode (SHE). This indicates that lithium is a highly effective reducing agent, meaning it has a strong tendency to transform into Li+.

On the other hand, fluorine (F) exhibits a remarkably high standard potential of 2.87 V vs SHE. This suggests that the oxidized form, F_2 gas, is an extremely potent oxidizing agent, exhibiting a strong inclination to become F-.

Theoretically, these observations imply that a Li–F_2 battery could have a theoretical cell voltage approximately around 5.91 V. And this is not a feasible pair for several reasons, falling beyond the scope of this guide, focused on viable pairs.

In the following points, material potentials are understood in their half-cell form, so the total cell voltage is the gap between both, being the most exploited to date lithium (-3V) and carbon (+1V).

Construction: a laminated approach

Some common materials used for electrode collector substrates are:

- Aluminum (Al) Foil
- Copper (Cu) Foil
- Carbon - Graphite Foil (C_{gr} or Gr)
- Nickel (Ni) Foil & Foam
- Stainless Steel Foil & Foam

The most common electrode collector substrate for anode in lithium-based cells is copper. It has good electrical conductivity and corrosion resistance and is an industrial commodity. Both nickel and copper have high electronic conductivity and good stability against lithium metal. They also have good compatibility with the roll-to-roll process.

Aluminum has lower specific gravity, lower electrical resistivity and higher heat conductivity than other metals such as copper or nickel. Also, aluminum does not dissolve in high action potential levels in non-aqueous electrolyte solutions such as in lithium-ion batteries. These properties make aluminum a good choice to be used as cathode collector in lithium ion batteries

Typical film thicknesses for separator film are 15microns, for copper film 10±4 microns, and aluminum film 25±15 microns, while typical coat weights for anode/cathode coatings are 1-5 kg/m2 per side. However, these values may vary depending on the application and design and can reach 4 microns for copper film and down to 8 microns for aluminum. Collectors are also surface treated to maximize adherence and conductivity with binders and load substrates. Some common materials used for coating lithium cathodes include aluminum oxide (Al_2O_3), polypyrrole (PPY), magnesium oxide (MgO), etc. Some common methods used for coating include atomic layer deposition (ALD), chemical vapor deposition (CVD), spray pyrolysis, etc. The coating thickness may vary from nanometers to micrometers depending on the material and method. For example, a coating thickness of 1 nm for Al_2O_3 using ALD, a coating thickness of 10-30 nm for PPY using CVD or a coating thickness of <1 wt% for MgO using ALD, which corresponds to about 0.5-1 μm assuming a density of 3.58 g/cm3 for MgO.

Anode mass loading can be in the range of 2±1 mg/cm2 for LiC_6, or 5±4 mg/cm2 for graphite (>30 microns per side). Cathode loadings are in the range of 25±15 mg/cm2 for NMC 811 (>50 microns thick per side).

Conductive binders are a must to hold the active material particles within the electrode of a lithium-ion battery together and maintain a strong connection between the electrode and the contacts. They also help form a good particle dispersion in solvent or water, aid in film formation, and resist electrolyte swelling. Water is a good, polar solvent at this stage, and it has a high specific heat among other undesirable properties.

Some of the most common binders for anode are Styrene-Butadiene Rubber (SBR) and Polyvinylidene Fluoride (PVDF). These binders are widely used because they have good adhesion, flexibility, and stability. However, they also have some drawbacks such as low conductivity, poor compatibility with silicon-based anodes, and environmental concerns. A new type of binder that has been recently investigated is polyamide imidazole (PAID) which has two functional groups for tight binding with silicon particles and carbon black. This binder can improve the performance and cycle life of silicon-based anodes in lithium-ion batteries. The typical composition range for cathode electrodes is 60–95% of active material and 5–25% of carbon and binder material. The exact ratio may vary depending on the specific materials used and their properties. Conductive additives such as carbon black or graphene have different conductivity and morphology which can affect the formation and stability of carbon-binder domain networks

The most common binders for cathode in lithium-ion batteries are Polyvinylidene Fluoride (PVDF), Styrene-Butadiene Rubber (SBR), and Hydrophilic binders. These binders are widely used because they have good adhesion, flexibility, and stability with various cathode materials. However, they also have some drawbacks such as low conductivity, high cost, environmental concerns, and need for toxic solvents. A new type of binder that has been recently explored is conducting polymer such as PEDOT:PSS which can improve the conductivity and performance of cathode electrodes. However, conducting polymer binders still need to be mixed with non-conductive binders and carbon additives to fabricate electrodes.

Some active materials such as NMC or LFP have different particle sizes and shapes which can affect the packing density and porosity of the electrode. A typical binder ratio for NMC cathodes is 5% by weight. However, this ratio may vary depending on specific materials used and their properties. For example, some binders such as Polyvinylidene Fluoride (PVDF) or Styrene-Butadiene Rubber (SBR) require more solvent than others such as Carboxymethyl Cellulose (CMC) or Sodium Alginate (SA) which can affect viscosity and coating thickness of slurry.

Increasing the anode/cathode mass loadings can improve the salt adsorption capacity and charge efficiency of capacitive deionization cells. However, there is also a trade-off between increasing the electrode thickness and reducing the diffusion rate of ions, which causes high internal resistance.

Binders: a scaffold for better performance

Binders are materials that are used to hold the active material particles together and in contact with the current collector in lithium cell anodes. Binders also provide mechanical strength and elasticity to cope with the volume changes during cycling.

Some of the common binders used in lithium cell anodes are Styrene-Butadiene Rubber (SBR) and Polyvinylidene Fluoride (PVDF)1. SBR is a water-based binder that has good adhesion and flexibility, but low thermal stability. PVDF is a solvent-based binder that has high thermal stability and electrochemical stability, but poor adhesion and flexibility.

There are also some novel binders that have been developed to improve the performance of silicon anodes, which have high capacity but also large volume expansion. These binders form a 3D network structure that can accommodate the volume changes and enhance the electrical conductivity of silicon anodes. Some examples of these binders are polyacrylic acid (PAA), carboxymethyl cellulose (CMC), and alginate.

The proportion of binders used in anode may depend on the type of binder and the type of active material. For example, using 5 wt% of PAA binder for silicon-based anodes, 1–3 wt% of different binders for silicon nanoparticles-based anodes or 1–2 wt% of PAA-PDA blended binder for silicon-based anodes.

Binders also affect the porosity, wettability, and stability of the cathode. Some of the common binders used in lithium cell cathodes are Polyvinylidene Fluoride (PVDF) and Polytetrafluoroethylene (PTFE). These are solvent-based binders that have good mechanical strength and electrochemical stability but require toxic solvents and high temperature for processing.

There are also some aqueous binders that have been developed to improve the sustainability and performance of lithium cell cathodes. These binders use water as a solvent instead of organic solvents, which reduces environmental impact and cost. Some examples of these binders are Carboxymethyl Cellulose (CMC), Styrene-Butadiene Rubber (SBR), Polyacrylic Acid (PAA), and Sodium Alginate (SA).

The proportion of binders used in cathode may depend on the type of binder and the type of active material. For example, using 4–12 wt% of PVDF binder for $LiCoO_2$-based cathodes or used 5 wt% of PTFE binder for $Li-O_2$-based cathodes.

PEO, PAN and PMMA are polymers that can be used as binders or electrolytes in lithium batteries. For reference only, 5 wt% of PEO binder for $Li-O_2$-based cathodes, 10–20 wt% of PAN binder for Li-S-based cathodes or 10–15 wt% of PMMA binder for $LiFePO_4$-based cathodes. Some innovations develop polymer film by trapping tribasic gel polymer electrolyte (GPE) blending PEO, PS and PMMA (1:1:1 wt ratio) achieving high ionic conductivity of 2.3×10^{-3} S cm−1 at room temperature and good electrochemical stability up to 4.8 V. High temperature resistance is also a challenge.

Cathode: the natural attractor

Lithium is held to the cathode mostly by a metal oxide layer that acts as a host for lithium ions. The metal oxide can vary depending on the type of lithium-based battery, but some common examples are cobalt oxide, iron phosphate, manganese oxide, nickel manganese cobalt oxide, and nickel cobalt aluminum oxide. The goal for such metal oxide combinations is to build a scaffold structure capable to de-insert lithium when a small voltage is applied and strong enough to not let the lithium ions get dissolved back into the electrolyte once inserted. These metal oxides have different properties that affect the performance and safety of the battery.

When lithium ions move in or out of the cathode, they change its electrical charge. To balance this charge, electrons must move through an external circuit that connects the cathode and the anode. This is how electric current is generated by a lithium-ion battery. For instance, NMC cathodes are lithium nickel manganese cobalt oxide cathodes that are commonly used in commodity cells. They are derived from solid solutions between $LiCoO_2$, $LiMnO_2$, and $LiNiO_2$. During discharge, lithium ions move from the anode to the NMC cathode through the electrolyte. The most common ternary NMC cathode undergoes a redox reaction where it accepts electrons from the external circuit and releases oxygen ions. Initial proportions were 111, later 523, 622, 811 and today 9.5.5 are under research. There are four main types of ternary materials in lithium-based cells:

- NCA: lithium nickel cobalt aluminum oxide ($LiNiCoAlO_2$)
- NCM: lithium nickel cobalt manganese oxide ($LiNiCoMnO_2$)
- LCO: lithium cobalt oxide ($LiCoO_2$)
- NMO: lithium nickel manganese oxide ($LiNiMnO_2$)

The opposite process happens when a lithium-ion battery is charged. The electrons are pulled from the cathode to the anode through an external circuit, and lithium ions follow them inside the battery.

To name a few of the mechanisms used to store lithium ions in cathode materials for lithium-ion batteries are:

- Intercalation: The insertion of lithium ions into the crystal structure of a host material without changing its structure. Examples are $LiCoO_2$, $LiMn_2O_4$ and $LiNi_{0.8}Co_{0.15}Al_{0.05}5O_2$.
- Conversion: The reaction of lithium with an oxide, sulfide or nitride to form metal nanoparticles embedded in a matrix of Li_2O, Li_2S or Li_3N. Examples are FeF_3, CuO and TiS_2.
- Bipolar charge storage: The simultaneous occurrence of n-type and p-type doping/de-doping mechanisms involving electrolyte ions such as $Li+$ and PF_6-. Examples are polymerized anthraquinone and poly(anthraquinonyl sulfide).
- Corrosion: The oxidation of a carbon cathode current collector/catalyst by high voltages during recharge. This mechanism leads to electrode degradation and poor performance. Examples are carbon nanotubes and graphene.

Advantages and disadvantages of each mechanism:

- Intercalation: Advantages are high energy density, low self-discharge rate and zero to low memory effect. Disadvantages are high cost, safety issues and limited cycle life.
- Conversion: Advantages are high capacity, low cost and diversity. Disadvantages are large volume change, poor reversibility and low coulombic efficiency.
- Bipolar charge storage: Advantages are high capacity, fast charge-discharge rates and light weight. Disadvantages are complex synthesis methods, compatibility issues and optimization challenges.
- Corrosion: This mechanism has no advantages but only disadvantages such as electrode degradation, poor performance and safety hazards.

In general, as the cathode potential is increased, the insertion potential becomes higher than before per each ion inserted, displaying a sort of exponential curve.

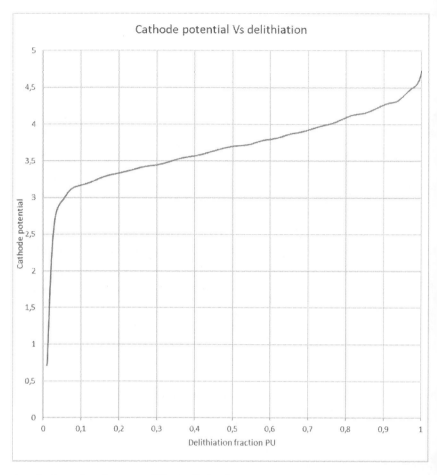

In all electrodes, there are different limits from useable capacity and theoretical capacity. While the raw material may have a capacity from 0 to 100%, not all can be used in that range to prevent irreversible damage.

Cell chemistry	Maximum capacity (mAh/g)	Reversible capacity (mAh/g)
LCO	274	145
NMC811	280	190
NCA	279	190
LFP	170	150

LMFP	140	110
Cgr-anode	372	325
LTO-anode	175	165
Silicon-anode	3578	708

The reversible capacity is the amount of charge that can be extracted from the electrode after the first cycle. It is usually lower than the initial capacity due to irreversible reactions that occur during the first cycle. The values are approximate and may vary depending on the experimental conditions and the battery design.

Vanadium oxide is a conversion-type anode material that can offer high capacity (1000 mAh/g) and good rate capability due to its multiple oxidation states and fast electron transfer. However, vanadium oxide also has drawbacks such as poor energy density, large volume change, poor cycling stability and high irreversible capacity which makes it not suitable for portable or mobile applications and are left out of scope.

The role of Nickel in cathode

Nickel is one of the transition metals that can be used in cathodes to compensate for the charge when lithium ions move in or out of the cathode. In lithium-ion batteries, Nickel (Ni) typically uses two oxidation states: Ni^{2+} and Ni^{4+}. During charging, Ni^{2+} ions in the cathode are oxidized to Ni^{4+}, which increases the cathode potential and allows lithium ions to be extracted from the anode and inserted into the cathode. During discharging, Ni^{4+} ions in the cathode are reduced to Ni^{2+}, which lowers the cathode potential and allows lithium ions to be released from the cathode and inserted into the anode. This reversible oxidation-reduction reaction involving Ni^{2+} and Ni^{4+} ions is what makes Nickel-based cathode materials such as NCA, NCO, NMC, and NMO attractive for use in lithium-ion batteries.

Nickel can also increase the energy density and reduce the cost of cathodes compared to other metals such as cobalt. For reference only, Ni increases the specific energy by 80Wh/kg per each unit of Mn replaced (boosting voltage) and Mn increases the specific energy by 30Wh/kg per each unit of Co replaced (boosting voltage). However, nickel also has some drawbacks such as lower thermal stability, accelerated degradation over cycle life and higher risk of fire, therefore needing other complementary elements to maintain a reasonable stability and cycle life.

The role of Manganese in cathode

Manganese is another transition metal that can be used in cathodes to compensate for the charge when lithium ions move in or out of the cathode. In lithium-ion batteries, manganese (Mn) typically uses three oxidation states: Mn^{2+}, Mn^{3+}, and Mn^{4+}. Manganese-based cathode materials such as $LiMn_2O_4$ spinel and $LiMnO_2$ layered oxide can reversibly intercalate lithium ions by changing their oxidation states between Mn3+ and Mn4+. During charging, Mn3+ ions in the cathode are oxidized to Mn4+, which increases the cathode potential and allows lithium ions to be extracted from the anode and inserted into the cathode. During discharging, Mn4+ ions in the cathode are reduced to Mn3+, which lowers the cathode potential and allows lithium ions to be released from the cathode and inserted into the anode. In some cases, manganese can also be reduced to Mn2+ under certain conditions, but this is usually not desirable as it can lead to irreversible capacity loss and performance degradation.

Manganese can also improve the safety and cost of cathodes compared to other metals such as cobalt. However, manganese also has some drawbacks such as halving the capacity over Cobalt, poor cycle life and thermal stability due to its weak bonding with oxygen. It also dissolves at higher temperatures and cycling.

The role of Cobalt in cathode

Cobalt oxides are another type of transition metal oxides that can be used in cathodes to compensate for the charge when lithium ions move in or out of the cathode. In lithium-ion batteries, cobalt (Co) typically uses two oxidation states: Co3+ and Co4+.

Cobalt-based cathode materials such as $LiCoO_2$ and $LiNiCoAlO_2$ (NCA) can intercalate lithium ions by changing the oxidation state of Co ions between Co3+ and Co4+. During charging, Co3+ ions in the cathode are oxidized to Co4+, which increases the cathode potential and allows lithium ions to be extracted from the anode and inserted into the cathode. During discharging, Co4+ ions in the cathode are reduced to Co3+, which lowers the cathode potential and allows lithium ions to be released from the cathode and inserted into the anode.

The reversible oxidation-reduction reaction involving Co3+ and Co4+ ions is what makes cobalt-based cathode materials attractive for use in lithium-ion batteries due to their high energy density and stability. Cobalt oxides can also provide stable high operation voltage, superior electronic conductivity, and high compaction density for cathodes. However, cobalt oxides are also expensive, scarce, and have environmental and ethical issues associated with their mining.

The role of Aluminum in cathode

Aluminum can replace some of the transition metals (such as nickel, cobalt, and manganese) in the layered structure of lithium cathodes. Aluminum can improve the electrochemical performance of Ni-rich (M) metal-oxide $LiNi_xCo_yM_{1-x-y}O_2$ (NCM; M=Mn, Al) cathodes by increasing the specific capacity, coulombic efficiency, and rate capability. This is because aluminum can reduce the lattice strain, structural integrity and microcracks in the cathode structure during cycling mitigating volume expansion.

It can also degrade the electrochemical performance of $LiCoO_2$ (LCO) cathodes by increasing the impedance and decreasing the lithium ion conductivity while improve the thermal stability. This is because aluminum can form a thick and dense protective Al_2O_3 layer on the cathode surface that blocks the lithium ion transport and prevents corrosion, oxidation, and Ni_2+ ion dissolution. This can enhance the safety and durability of lithium batteries. *However, too much aluminum can also have negative effects.* For instance, aluminum can increase the charge transfer resistance and decrease the lithium diffusion coefficient of the cathodes. This can lower the rate capability and energy density of the cathodes.

A small amount of aluminum (x = 0.01) can improve the capacity retention and thermal stability of $Li[Ni_{0.92-x}Co_{0.04}Mn_{0.04}Al_{2x}]O_2$ cathodes by forming a protective Al_2O_3 layer on the surface. Too much aluminum (x = 0.05) can degrade the specific capacity and rate capability of the cathodes by increasing the charge transfer resistance and decreasing the lithium diffusion coefficient.

The optimal amount of aluminum substitution depends on several factors, such as the composition, structure, and desired performance of the lithium cathodes.

Therefore Aluminum (Al) is not typically used as a cathode material in lithium-ion batteries, so it does not undergo oxidation-reduction reactions in the same way that cathode materials do. However, aluminum can be used as an anode material in some types of lithium-ion batteries, such as lithium-ion capacitors or hybrid supercapacitors. During charging of these types of batteries, aluminum atoms in the anode lose electrons and become Al3+ ions, which are then attracted to the negative electrode. During discharging, the Al3+ ions in the electrolyte are reduced to aluminum atoms at the anode, which then release electrons to the external circuit. The reversible oxidation-reduction reaction involving aluminum ions and aluminum atoms is what enables the energy storage and release in these types of batteries.

The role of Phosphate (PO_4) in cathode

Olivines are a family of phosphate-based anode materials (such as $LiFePO_4$, $LiMnPO_4$ and $LiCoPO_4$) that have high thermal stability, environmental friendliness and safety. However, olivine materials also have low conductivity, low capacity (around 150 mAh/g) and high working potential (around 3 V vs. Li+/Li).

Phosphate is a replacement for oxides (O_2) and it is mostly known for its associations with Iron. Iron phosphate is a type of cathode material that can be used in lithium-ion or sodium-ion batteries. It has some advantages over other cathode materials, such as low cost, high safety, long cycle life, and environmental friendliness.

LFP cathodes are known for their stability and durability. However, its lower voltage and lower energy density made them less attractive than ternary cathodes. To boost their voltage, Mn is added to the mixture to form Lithium Manganese Iron Phosphate cells. Due to the good lattice stability of the olivine structure type, the cycling performance of both LFP and LMFP is better than that of ternary.

$LiMn_xFe_{1-x}PO_4$ combines the high safety and long-life cycle of $LiFePO_4$ and the high energy density of $LiMnPO_4$. Restricting factors for achieving high-rate performance of LMFP include its dual voltage plateaus (typical from Mn), low electronic conductivity and Li+ diffusion coefficient and optimization of the Fe/Mn ratio.

LMFP is matching the LFP capacity at 170mAh/g, but the voltage platform of lithium iron phosphate is only 3.4 V, while lithium manganese iron phosphate can reach 4.1 V due to the higher redox potential of manganese ions Mn3+/Mn2+, which makes the energy density of LMFP increase up to 20% at the same specific capacity.

The low temperature performance of LMFP is better than that of LFP which has poor low temperature performance with a capacity retention rate at 60% at -20°C, while the capacity retention rate of LMFP can reach about 75% at -20°C.

LMFP with its olivine structure is more stable and safer than ternary material with a layered structure. Strong covalent P–O bonds in the tetrahedral PO_4^{3-} anion stabilizes the oxygen atom and inhibits oxygen loss which make LMFP more stable during charging and discharging and Thermal Runaway. However, due to the poor high temperature performance of manganese element, the safety performance of LMFP is slightly worse than that of LFP, but both are considered safer than ternary materials.

The role of Sulfur in cathode

Sulfur is a key component of lithium-sulfur batteries (Li-S batteries), which are a type of rechargeable battery that have a high specific energy. Sulfur atoms form rings that react with lithium ions and release energy. Sulfur can store more lithium than other materials, such as cobalt, which makes Li-S batteries lighter, safer, more sustainable and cheaper.

During discharge, the lithium metal anode releases lithium ions and electrons to the external circuit.

During charge, the lithium ions and electrons return to the anode and deposit as metallic lithium on the anode surface.

The anode also reacts with some of the polysulfides that diffuse from the cathode and forms a passivation layer of lithium sulfide or lithium polysulfide on its surface. This layer can protect the anode from further corrosion but also increase its resistance and reduce its capacity, while evolving as the cell ages.

Some of the challenges of Li-S batteries are:

- The shuttle effect of polysulfide intermediates, which are soluble compounds that form during the charge and discharge cycles and cause active material loss, capacity degradation and short cycle life.
- The poor electronic conductivity of sulfur and lithium sulfide, which are the charge and discharge products of the cathode and limit the material utilization and reaction kinetics.
- The instability of the lithium metal anode, which can form dendrites that pierce through the separator and cause internal short circuits or fire hazards

The anode can be made of:

- A lithium metal anode that releases electrons and lithium ions during discharge.
- A sulfur-carbon composite cathode that absorbs electrons and lithium ions and forms lithium sulfide during discharge.

- An electrolyte that contains dissolved polysulfides, which are intermediate products of the sulfur reduction reaction.

And therefore, it sets another paradigm which is left out of scope for this compilation.

The role of Yttrium in LFP cathode

Yttrium is added to LFP cathodes to improve the electrochemical performance of the cathode by enhancing the structure via a surface gradient doping. The addition of yttrium can improve the rate capability, the capacity retention, the potential, thermal, and cycling stability of LFP cathodes.

Yttrium doping ranges in 0,1-0,5 wt% can also improve the electronic conductivity of LFP cathodes thanks to the modified surface. Some methods used are co-precipitation and solid-state reactions.

Anode, the holder

The role of the anode in a lithium-based cell is to store lithium ions that come from the cathode during charging and release them during discharge. It also passes the currents through an external circuit via its current collector. The anode plays a vital role in defining the cycle life of a lithium-based cell.

Some of the mechanisms used to store lithium ions in anode materials for lithium-ion batteries are:

- Intercalation: The insertion of lithium ions into the crystal structure of a host material without changing its structure. Examples are graphite and $Li_4Ti_5O_{12}$.
- Alloying: The formation of a new compound between lithium and another element that can accommodate a large amount of lithium. Examples are silicon, tin and germanium.
- Conversion: The reaction of lithium with an oxide, sulfide or nitride to form metal nanoparticles embedded in a matrix of Li_2O, Li_2S or Li_3N. Examples are Fe_3O_4, Co_3O_4 and MoS_2.
- Hybrid: A combination of two or more mechanisms mentioned above. Examples are $ZnTiO_3$-CeO_2 and Si-Cu.

Advantages and disadvantages of each mechanism:

Mechanism	Advantages	Disadvantages
Intercalation	high reversibility, good cycle life and stability	low capacity, limited lithium insertion sites and requiring crystallographic structural changes
Alloying	high capacity, low cost and abundance of base materials	large volume expansion, poor cycling stability and low electrical conductivity
Conversion	high capacity, low cost and diversity	large volume expansion, poor reversibility and low coulombic

		efficiency
Hybrid	improved performance by combining different mechanisms such as higher capacity, better stability and enhanced conductivity	complex synthesis methods, compatibility issues and optimization challenges

The future trends are pointing towards higher stability and energy density as different materials have different advantages and disadvantages depending on the application and performance criteria. Some candidates for stable anode materials for lithium-ion batteries are:

- Graphite: This is the most widely used anode material due to its low cost, high capacity, long cycle life and low working potential (0.1 V vs. Li+/Li).
- Silicon: This is an alloying-type anode material that can achieve very high capacity due to its ability to form Li_xSi alloys with various compositions.

The role of Graphite in anode

The role of graphite in anode is to act as a host structure for the reversible intercalation of lithium ions and is to date the most extended material thanks to its reduced costs and low volume change as well as reasonable conductivity. Intercalation is the process by which a mobile ion or molecule is reversibly incorporated into vacant sites in a crystal lattice. The intercalation stresses the lattices and causes a slight expansion of 13.2% from totally depleted to fully lithiated, although never must experience those extreme states.

Graphite has a high theoretical capacity of 372 mAh/g when forming LiC_6 and an appropriate lithiation/de-lithiation potential, making it a common material for lithium-ion battery. However, graphite also suffers from safety issues such as easy lithium dendrite formation (when its insertion potential gets above the lithium metal overpotential threshold) and electrolyte decomposition at very low voltages.

Synthetic graphite requires a lower insertion overpotential as natural graphite is slightly more compact. Therefore, the former is more appropriate for high power applications and the latter for high capacity, where ions mobility is less of a constraint. However, a correct blending is often the benchmark.

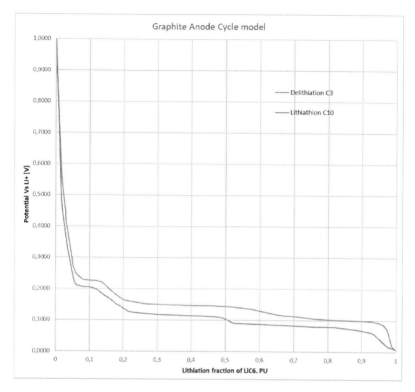

Graphite carbon undergoes several transitions in a full charge discharge cycle of a lithium-ion battery. These transitions include:

- The formation of a solid electrolyte interphase (SEI) layer on the graphite surface during the first charge cycle, which protects the graphite from further electrolyte decomposition but also increases the internal resistance and reduces the capacity.
- The intercalation of lithium ions into different stages of graphite, such as LiC_6, LiC_{12} and LiC_{18}, depending on the voltage and lithium concentration. These stages have different crystal structures and lattice parameters.
- The lithiophobic-to-lithiophilic transition on the graphite surface at high potentials, which can enhance the kinetics of lithium diffusion and improve the fast-charging performance.
- The transformation of graphite into other carbonaceous compounds such as amorphous carbon or turbostratic carbon due to mechanical stress, side reactions or overcharging. These transformations can degrade the electrode structure and performance.

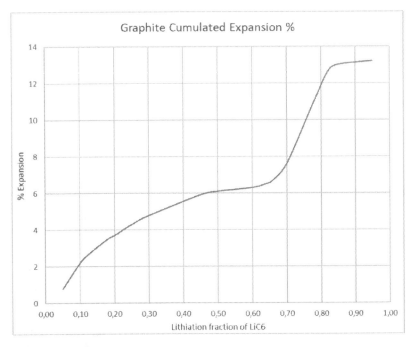

LiC6 starts appearing at 60% lithiation. Beyond 85% there is little effect on volume, but

And why is not graphene used instead? It turns out that the higher the crystallinity, the more edges are exposed, and faster degradation occurs during cycling. Therefore, nanostructured grains are engineered, either made of crystalline graphite coated with a layer of amorphous carbon or via curved (spheroid) graphite grains.

The role of Hard Carbon in anode

Hard carbon is a type of carbonaceous anode material that has a high capacity and a low potential for alkali metal-ion batteries. It is composed of a graphite-like crystallite structure and open horn-like crystallites. It is considered to be low cost, easy to synthesize, and sustainable

Hard carbon is not a common collector for lithium-based batteries because it faces some challenges such as:

- Low lithium storage capacity
- Poor rate and cycle performance
- Low initial Coulombic efficiency
- Unclear lithium storage mechanism

These challenges limit the practical application of hard carbon anodes for next-generation batteries.

The role of Silicon in anode

Silicon anodes are another type of anode material for lithium batteries that have a higher specific capacity than graphite. However, they also have some drawbacks such as:

- Large volume change during charging and discharging
- Instability of bulk and interfacial structures
- Cracking and disintegration, pulverization of the anode, mechanical properties

These problems affect the performance and life span of silicon anodes. Some possible solutions include using nanoparticles, composites, coatings, or additives to improve the stability and conductivity of silicon anode.

Silicon is better than graphite in anode in terms of energy capacity. Silicon can absorb more lithium than graphite and has a theoretical capacity of 4200 mAh/g, which is 10 times greater than graphite's 372 mAh/g. This means that silicon anodes can store more energy and deliver longer range for batteries. However, silicon also has some disadvantages such as volume expansion, structural instability, and electrolyte degradation

The difference in volume expansion between silicon and graphite is significant. Silicon expands almost 300% during the charging process, when lithium ions enter the anode. Graphite, on the other hand, expands only about 10% upon lithiation. This means that silicon anodes undergo more stress and deformation than graphite anodes during battery operation.

To overcome this challenge, researchers have developed silicon-graphite composite anodes that combine silicon with graphite to improve the stability and performance of the anode. The optimum amount of silicon in graphite anodes depends on various factors, such as:

- The type and size of silicon particles
- The method of mixing silicon with graphite
- The pre-lithiation process of the anode
- The cycling conditions of the battery

A silicon content of ~10 wt% within a silicon-graphite composite anode can achieve a high initial capacity of ~500 mAh/g and a stable cycle life over 100 cycles. Some commercial cells include up to 5 wt% Si.

The role of LTO in anode

LTO anode is a type of anode material that uses lithium titanate (LTO, $Li_4Ti_5O_{12}$) instead of graphite in lithium-ion batteries. LTO anodes have some advantages such as high-power density, long cycle life, fast charging capability, low self-discharge and low volume expansion. However, LTO anodes also have some drawbacks such as low energy density, high cost, and low operating voltage window. LTO can be used in combination with different cathode materials, depending on the desired performance and application of the battery.

Advantages	Drawbacks
- Higher thermal stability and safety	- Lower energy density and specific capacity
- Longer cycle life and shelf life	
- Faster charging and discharging	- Higher cost and weight
	- Lower nominal voltage
- Wider operating temperature range	

One of the reasons why LTO is more stable than carbon graphite is that it has a lower intercalation potential for lithium ions, which means it operates within the thermodynamic stability window of the electrolyte and avoids the formation of a complex SEI that can degrade the performance of carbon graphite. Another reason is that LTO has a spinel structure that can accommodate large volume changes during lithiation and delithiation without cracking or pulverizing.

The cycle life of an LTO based cell depends on various factors, such as temperature, charge and discharge rate, depth of discharge and initial state of health. LTO cells can last for 3000 to 7000 charge cycles before reaching 80% capacity at moderate C-rates. However, this number can be reduced to ~1000 cycles if the cells are charged and discharged at 55 °C instead of 25 °C room temperature.

Some of the most common cathode materials with LTO anode are:

- Lithium manganese oxide (LMO)
- Lithium nickel manganese cobalt oxide (NMC)
- Lithium iron phosphate (LFP)

These cathode materials have different characteristics, such as:

- LMO has high power density, low cost and good thermal stability.
- NMC has high energy density, good rate capability and moderate cost.
- LFP has high safety, long cycle life and environmental friendliness.

Generating voltage

By using the gap between Lithium metal and its stable compounds, a voltage can be extracted depending on the anode/cathode pairing. In the engineering world voltage is to height as electric charge is to volume. Figuring out the electrons as a viscous liquid (water, oil), is easy to find and visualize similarities.

The free potential vs lithium of a cathode material is a measure of its voltage when it is fully charged with lithium ions. Different cathode materials have different free potentials vs lithium, which affect their energy density and power density.

The averaged free potential vs lithium of some common cathode materials is:

- Lithium cobalt oxide (LCO): 4.2 V
- Lithium nickel cobalt aluminum oxide (NCA): 4.1 V
- Lithium nickel manganese cobalt oxide (NMC): 3.9 V

- Lithium manganese oxide (LMO): 3.8 V
- Lithium iron phosphate (LFP): 3.2 V
- Lithium manganese iron phosphate (LMFP): 3.6 V

The averaged free potential vs lithium of some common anode materials is:

- Lithium titanate (LTO): 1.5 V
- Graphite: 0.01 V
- Hard carbon: 0.01 V
- Silicon: 0.01 V

Therefore, an LFP/LTO will have a maximum voltage of about 1,7V on an average cell, despite having a massive increase in cyclability.

A summary of the specific energy, maximum voltage and cost of LCO, NCA, NMC, LMO, LFP and LMFP cathode materials for reference:

Chemistry	Wh/kg	Max Voltage	Avg Voltage	Cost
LCO	180±20	4.3	3.7	+++++
NCA	230±30	4.2	3.6	++++
NMC	125±25	4.0	3.7	++
LFP	105±20	3.6	3.2	+
LMFP	120±25	3.7	3.3	++
LNMO	160±20	4.8	4.1	+++

Electrode collectors serve as thin substrates that not only support the active materials but also conduct the electrons. The mass load, defined as the quantity of active material per unit area of the electrode, is another significant parameter. Adjusting these parameters can influence the performance of a lithium battery, making it suitable for various applications.

In the case of high power cells, there is a need for low mass load and high conductivity collectors. These collectors are typically thick to minimize internal resistance and heat generation, thereby enhancing the cell's power output. Conversely, high energy cells demand a high mass load and thin electrodes. This configuration increases the capacity and energy density, which are critical for long lasting applications.

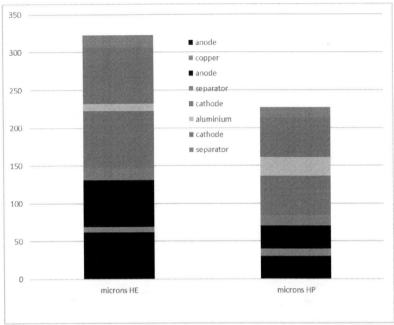

There are trade-offs between mass load, electrode thickness, the type of current collector, and other factors to optimize the battery for its intended type and functionality, mainly prioritizing High Energy (HE) or Power (HP).

1. When comparing cells with the same discharge rates the cell with thicker electrodes exhibits a higher and more uneven temperature response. These factors can accelerate the depletion of active material, leading to faster capacity fade.
2. Thicker electrodes result in a longer diffusion distance, which can cause more severe concentration polarization. This results in a higher internal resistance, which can lower power output and cause the discharge to stop earlier due to the cell reaching its minimum voltage sooner.
3. At high discharge rates, ohmic heating becomes the dominant factor, especially in cells with thick electrodes. This leads to a faster deterioration in the state of health of the battery.
4. Due to diffusion limitations and asymmetrical tabs, the electrochemical reactions occur unevenly within the cell with thick electrodes, particularly under high rates. This uneven distribution not only leads to the underutilization of active materials but also increases the thermal instability of the cell.

Making a cell alive

Formation

Once a battery is assembled, the materials need to have its first reactions until they reach some stability. As ions move way slower than electrons, the dynamic response (power) of cells is dictated by the lithium-ions mobility within the cell, and the results after formation display pretty much how it will behave in the future.

Cell formation is the process of charging and discharging the cell for the first time after injecting the electrolyte into it. This process forms a protective layer called SEI on the electrodes that enables the cell to store and release ions.

Battery cell formation is a critical step in battery manufacturing as it affects the performance, safety and lifetime of the cell. The formation process can take several days depending on the battery chemistry and requires precise control of current and voltage, often topping the material limits which will never again be pushed that far also in temperature and pressure.

The pre-lithiation stage in cell manufacturing is a process that involves adding extra lithium sources to the anode or the cathode of a lithium-ion battery before assembling the full cell. The purpose of this process is to mitigate the initial active lithium loss (ALL) that occurs in the first several cycles of charging and discharging, which reduces the first cycles Coulombic efficiency and the energy density of the battery. The pre-lithiation stage can also decrease the potential gap of the anode and increase the safety of the battery.

There are various pre-lithiation methods that have been developed, such as using lithium metal foil, lithium alloy foil, lithium powder, lithium salt solution, lithium ion source solution, lithiated carbon materials, lithiated transition metal oxides, and lithiated silicon materials. Each method has its own advantages and challenges in terms of cost, efficiency, scalability, and compatibility with different anode and cathode materials.

The benefits of pre-lithiating the anode or the cathode are mainly related to improving the energy density, cycle stability, and safety of the battery. Some of the specific benefits are:

- Pre-lithiating the anode can compensate for the active lithium loss that occurs during the formation of the SEI on the anode surface, which reduces the first Coulombic efficiency and the reversible capacity of the battery.
- Pre-lithiating the anode can lower the redox potential of the anode and increase the overall cell potential, which results in higher cell energy density and reduced electrode resistance.
- Pre-lithiating the anode can maintain a steady electrolyte conductivity by keeping the anion-cation concentration in the electrolyte mostly stable during cycling, which is crucial for cell efficiency and cyclability.
- Pre-lithiating the cathode can balance the ratio between cathode and anode and avoid over-lithiation or under-lithiation of either electrode, which can cause capacity fading, voltage decay, or thermal runaway.
- Pre-lithiating the cathode can reduce the polarization and impedance of the cathode and enhance its rate capability and cycling performance.

As per general criteria that can be used to evaluate the effectiveness of a pre-lithiation method are:

- The amount of extra lithium that can be added to the electrode without causing excess lithium or lithium dendrite formation.
- The uniformity and stability of the lithium distribution in the electrode and the electrolyte.

- The compatibility and reversibility of the lithium source with the electrode material and the electrolyte.
- The simplicity and controllability of the process and the equipment required.

Based on these criteria, some researchers have suggested that electrochemical pre-lithiation is an ideal method as it only puts lithium ions into the anode and leaves no other compound behind, while avoiding excess lithium or dendrite formation. However, this method may require a complex setup and a long time to achieve sufficient pre-lithiation.

Other methods, such as using sacrificial additives or pre-lithiated materials, may be more convenient and scalable, but they may also introduce impurities or side reactions that affect the battery performance and safety. Therefore, the best pre-lithiation method may depend on the specific application and design of the battery.

The amount of additional lithium that is added at pre-lithiation depends on the type of electrode material, the pre-lithiation method, and the desired performance of the battery. Generally, the amount of extra lithium should not exceed the capacity of the electrode, otherwise it may cause excess lithium or lithium dendrite formation that can affect the life and safety of the battery. Some examples of the amount of additional lithium that is added at pre-lithiation are:

- For graphite anodes, pre-lithiation with Li foil can provide about 100 mAh/g of extra lithium, while pre-lithiation with super-concentrated electrolyte can provide about 50 mAh/g.
- For silicon-based anodes, pre-lithiation with Li foil can provide about 1000 mAh/g of extra lithium, while pre-lithiation with Li_8ZrO_6 can provide about 550 mAh/g.
- For layered oxide cathodes, pre-lithiation with Li_2S can provide about 50 mAh/g of extra lithium, while pre-lithiation with Li_2O_2 can provide about 30 mAh/g

The optimal amount of additional lithium that is added at pre-lithiation may vary depending on the specific application and design of the battery. The goal is to balance the ratio between cathode and anode and compensate for the active lithium loss without compromising the battery performance and safety.

The SEI, a live component of the cell

The solid electrolyte interphase (SEI) is a thin layer that forms on the surface of the anode (the negative electrode) and cathode (positive electrode) of a battery mainly during the initial charge and discharge cycles. It is built from various compounds that result from the electrochemical reduction of the electrolyte (the liquid or gel that carries the ions between the electrodes have a potential window above of that lithium anode insertion potential), salts and other materials within the cell, and evolves along the cell life. Some of the electrolyte species that are consumed during lithium ion cell formation are $LiPF_6$, EC and DMC. Other of consumed compounds are lithium fluoride, lithium oxide, lithium carbonate, organic polymers and inorganic salts.

The SEI plays a crucial role in the performance, safety and lifetime of a battery as it affects the charge transfer kinetics and increase the internal resistance of the battery. On one hand, it protects the anode from further decomposition by blocking (slowing) unwanted side reactions between the anode active materials and the electrolyte and preserves the long-term cyclability of the battery. On the other hand, it allows lithium ions to pass through it and reach the anode during charging and discharging. There is no known polar solvent which can resist both reductive decomposition at 0.1V potential (underdischarge) and stability at 6V (overcharge, fast charge overpotential). In fact, current electrolyte potential window is set between 4.5V (oxidation) and 0.5V (reduction). So the electrolyte will for sure react with the anode and with cathode under specific circumstances.

However, if the SEI is not stable or uniform, it can cause problems such as increased internal resistance, capacity loss, self-discharge and thermal runaway. Therefore, controlling and optimizing the formation and properties of the SEI is essential for improving battery performance. For instance, mixing carbon traces in the LFP anode slurry allows the formation of a quality SEI which dramatically reduces interface diffusion resistance.

As an active cell component, its composition and properties change upon current, temperature and other stress factors along the cell lifecycle, being most of the reactions non-reversible, i.e. the graphene edge surface increase, with its catalytic effect to consume electrolyte to form new SEI.

The species that are reduced to form the initial SEI are mainly lithium ions and electrolyte components. The formation of the SEI consumes some of the initial capacity of the battery as it reduces the amount of available lithium ions for intercalation into the anode. Hence, up to 15wt% of lithium salt and electrolyte excess is initially considered for the SEI formation or in pre-lithiation. In early developments, Vinylene Carbonate (VC) was used as a sacrificial solvent to enhance SEI formation

The amount of lithium that is lost during SEI formation depends on the type of anode material, the electrolyte composition, and the operating conditions of the battery. Generally, the amount of lithium that is lost during SEI formation is proportional to the surface area of the anode and inversely proportional to the thickness of the SEI layer. As a rule of thumb for lost lithium during SEI formation are:

- For graphite anodes, about 5-20% of the total lithium inventory of the cathode and electrolyte salt. This corresponds to about 50-200 mAh/g of lithium loss for a typical graphite anode with a capacity of 372 mAh/g.
- For silicon-based anodes, the amount of lithium lost during SEI formation is much higher than for graphite anodes, due to the large volume expansion and contraction of silicon during cycling. The amount of lithium loss can range from 300 to 1000 mAh/g for a silicon anode with a capacity of 4200 mAh/g.
- For lithium metal anodes, the amount of lithium loss during formation is also very high, due to the high reactivity and low stability of lithium metal. The amount of lithium loss can be as high as 1000 mAh/g for a lithium metal anode with a capacity of 3860 mAh/g.

The amount of lithium that is lost during SEI formation can affect the energy density, cycle life, and safety of the battery. There are different ways to minimize the lithium loss during SEI formation, depending on the type of anode material, the electrolyte composition, and the operating conditions of the battery as:

- Using anode materials that have a low surface area and a stable SEI layer, such as graphite or lithium titanate.

- Using electrolyte additives that can enhance the stability and selectivity of the SEI layer, such as vinylene carbonate (VC), fluoroethylene carbonate, or lithium nitrate at low concentrations (2wt%).
- Using electrolyte solvents that can resist reduction and form a thin and uniform SEI layer, such as ethers or sulfones.
- Using electrolyte salts that can reduce the solubility and mobility of lithium ions in the electrolyte, such as lithium bis(fluorosulfonyl)imide or lithium bis(oxalato)borate.
- Optimizing the operating temperature and voltage of the battery to avoid excessive SEI growth and lithium plating.
- Pre-lithiating the anode to compensate for the initial active lithium loss and reduce the anode overpotential.

These methods can help reduce the amount of lithium that is lost during SEI formation and improve the energy density, capacity retention, and safety of the battery. But not all work the same for everything. For example, VC is an effective additive for a stable SEI on Cgr anodes, while in combination with LNMO cathodes ($LiNi_{0.5}Mn_{1.5}O_4$), VC drops cell performance significantly.

The SEI evolution is due to the anode expansion and contraction during cycling. The anode cracks and new electrolyte and salt is consumed to heal the induced creeks, sealing the freshly exposed area. This reduces the amount of lithium and electrolyte available, making it viscous. Another mechanism is thickening of SEI, which traps more active ions and increases the resistance too. Capturing ions reduces the capacity while increase in resistance reduces the operating potential and the dynamic power and thermal output of the cell.

The electrolyte: a conductive salt and solvent mix

The electrolyte composition varies among different battery chemistries depending on the type of electrodes, the operating voltage and temperature range, and the desired performance characteristics. The electrolyte typically consists of a solvent (an engineered blend of polar liquids that dissolves the salt, such as ethylene carbonate or dimethyl carbonate) and a salt (a compound that dissociates into ions in the solvent, such as lithium hexafluorophosphate - $LiPF_6$ or lithium perchlorate).

Some examples of commonly used solvents are ethylene carbonate (EC), dimethyl carbonate (DMC), diethyl carbonate (DEC), propylene carbonate (PC), ethyl methyl carbonate (EMC) and gamma-butyrolactone (GBL). To mention commonly used salts as lithium hexafluorophosphate ($LiPF_6$), lithium perchlorate (LiClO4), lithium tetrafluoroborate ($LiBF_4$), lithium bis(trifluoromethanesulfonyl)imide (LiTFSI) and lithium bis(oxalato)borate (LiBOB).

Polarity helps to dissolve lithium salts, and it has to be strong enough to keep the suspension and weak enough to let the ions move freely through the electrolyte and separator. Cyclic esters display a much higher polarity than linear esters, at the expense of being more stable and requiring a higher overpotential to let the ions go. Some examples of high-polarity electrolytes are those that contain high-polarity solvents such as ethylene carbonate (EC), dimethyl carbonate (DMC), or propylene carbonate (PC).

Linear solvents	Cyclic solvents

Ethylene carbonate (EC)	Propylene carbonate (PC)
Diethyl carbonate (DEC)	Ethyl methyl carbonate (EMC)
Dimethyl carbonate (DMC)	Fluoroethylene carbonate (FEC)
Methyl propionate (MP)	Vinylene carbonate (VC)
Fluorinated diethoxyethane (FDEE)	Fluorinated propylene carbonate (FPC)
	Gamma-butyrolactone (GBL)

Lithium salt is the supplier of lithium ions in the electrolyte. $LiPF_6$ (lithium hexafluorophosphate) is the most common lithium salt at present. The development of new lithium salts $LiBF_4$ (lithium tetrafluoroborate), LiBOB (lithium dioxalate borate), LiDFOB (lithium oxalate diborate), LiFSI (Lithium bisfluorosulfonimide), LiTFSI (lithium bistrifluoromethylsulfonimide), $LiPF_2O_2$ (lithium difluorophosphate) and LiDTI (lithium 4,5-dicyano-2-trifluoromethylimidazolium) has also received increasing attention from researchers. The advantages and disadvantages of the comparison are as follows:

Table 1. Comparison of advantages and disadvantages of various lithium salts.

Lithium salt	Advantage	Disadvantage
$LiPF_6$	It has suitable solubility and high ionic conductivity in non-aqueous solvent. It forms a stable passivation film on the surface of the Al foil current collector. And also a stable SEI film can be formed on the surface of the graphite electrode in synergy with the carbonate solvent.	The thermal stability is poor and the decomposition reaction is easy to occur.
$LiBF_4$	$LiBF_4$ has wide operating temperature range, good high temperature stability and excellent low temperature performance. It can enhance the film forming ability of electrolyte on the electrode and inhibit the corrosion of Al foil.	The ionic conductivity is low, which has great limitations. It is often associated with lithium salt with high conductivity.
LiBOB	LiBOB has higher conductivity, wider electrochemical window, good thermal stability, better cycle stability, passivation protection for positive Al foil current collector	Low solubility, and almost insoluble in solvent of low dielectric constant.
LiDFOB	LiDFOB has good film formation, good low temperature performance, good compatibility with battery positive electrode, can form a passivation film on the surface of Al foil, and inhibit the oxidation of electrolyte.	High price
LiFSI	LiFSI has high conductivity, low water sensitivity and good thermal stability, anti-corrosion capacities, enlarging battery life and reducing discharge at ow temperatures.	Corrosion potential of Al foil is 4.2V.
LiTFSI	LiTFSI has higher solubility and conductivity, thermal decomposition temperature exceeds 360 °C, and is difficult to hydrolyze.	When the voltage is higher than 3.7V, it will seriously corrode the Al current collector.
$LiPF_2O_2$	$LiPF_2O_2$ has good low temperature performance; beneficial to reduce the interface impedance of the battery (quick charge) and effectively improve the cycle performance of the battery. Stable.	The solubility is low.
LiDTI	LiDTI has better thermodynamic stability; it can be stably existed at 4.5V and has a high lithium ion migration number, which can meet the charging and discharging requirements of commercial cathode materials.	High synthesis requirements

What are the characteristics of an ideal electrolyte lithium salt?
1. Low dissociation energy and high solubility: low dissociation can ensure the electrolyte formed after the dissolution of lithium salt has high conductivity, thus achieving high C-rate; high solubility ensures enough lithium ion in electrolyte transmission.
2. Better stability: When the battery is operated under high voltage and high temperature, the lithium salt will not react with other components.
3. Good SEI film forming properties to ensure that the electrolyte is not continuously consumed during subsequent cycles.
4. Good passivation of Aluminium current collector to prevent corrosion of Al foil at high voltage.
5. Low cost, non-toxic and pollution-free.

The electrolyte has an important influence on battery cycle life, rate performance, applicable temperature and safety. Electrolyte polarity determines the solvation structure of lithium ions, which influences the interfacial reactions between the electrolyte and the electrodes. A low-polarity electrolyte can reduce the formation of organic components on the anode surface, which can improve the cycling stability and coulombic efficiency of a lithium cell. However, a low-polarity electrolyte may also have lower ionic conductivity and higher viscosity than a high-polarity electrolyte, which can limit its application in high-power lithium cells.

Lithium salts, as providers of lithium ions in the electrolyte, significantly affect the performance of the electrolyte. $LiPF_6$ is currently the most widely used lithium salt, but its thermal stability is poor and sensitive to water. Therefore, finding new lithium salts with excellent performance has become the focus of current research. Although new lithium salts such as $LiBF_4$, LiBOB, LiTFSI, LiFSI, $LiPF_2O_2$, and LiTDI can avoid the disadvantages of $LiPF_6$, they have problems in electrical conductivity, corrosion and price. Therefore, no lithium salt has been able to completely replace $LiPF_6$.

The choice of solvent and salt depends on several factors such as conductivity, viscosity, stability, compatibility, toxicity and cost. For example, EC has high stability but low conductivity and high viscosity; DMC has high conductivity but low stability; $LiPF_6$ has high conductivity but low thermal stability; $LiClO_4$ has high conductivity but high safety risk. Trimethyl phosphate (TMP) is used as a solvent because it is identified as a good flame retardant and has high oxidative stability and low viscosity.

A common electrolyte composition for lithium-ion batteries with graphite anode and $LiCoO_2$ cathode is 1 M $LiPF_6$ in EC:DMC:DEC with a volume ratio of 1:1:123. A common electrolyte composition for lithium-sulfur batteries with carbon-sulfur composite cathode is 0.5 M LiTFSI in DME:DOL with a volume ratio of 1:1.

New trends try to merge functionalities with Room Temperature Ionic Liquids (RTIL), which are salts that melt at temperatures below 100°C to perform both roles simultaneously and remain still at low TRL.

The separator: a must-have unpolluted

A separator is the critical thin layer of material from 10 to 25 microns that separates the anode and cathode of a battery and prevents a short circuit. It physically separates the positive and negative electrodes while allowing the flow of lithium ions. It is typically made of a porous polymer material that can withstand the harsh chemical environment of the battery and maintain its structural integrity over the lifetime of the battery. The pores must be large enough to allow a lithium ion pass-through but not the entire lithium atom, forcing the overhead electron to circulate via the collectors and external electric circuit.

A thinner separator can increase the energy density of the battery but can also increase the risk of short circuits and thermal runaway if the battery is damaged or abused. A thicker separator can improve safety but can also reduce the energy density and power output of the battery due to massive increase in tortuosity. Tortuosity is a parameter that describes the complexity of the pore network in a porous material, such as a battery electrode or separator. It affects the transport properties of the liquid electrolyte in the pores, such as diffusivity and conductivity. The higher the tortuosity, the lower the effective transport properties and varies depending on the composition, morphology, and manufacturing process of the porous material. Tortuosity can be measured by different methods, such as electrochemical impedance spectroscopy (EIS), differential thermal analysis (DTA), or imaging analysis.

Porous polypropylene is a common separator compound in lithium cells. Separators can also be made of polyethylene, ceramic, glass fiber, or cellulose. Production methods comprise mechanical stretching of compact films and solvent-induced pore forming or combination of both.

Separator clogging in lithium-ion cells occurs when the pores of the separator become filled with solid deposits or particles, preventing the flow of lithium ions and leading to a reduction in battery performance or even failure. During the operation of the battery, various factors such as electrode degradation, electrolyte decomposition, or the formation of SEI can result in the deposition of solid particles or materials in the pores of the separator. This can reduce the effective surface area of the electrodes and limit the flow of lithium ions, leading to a reduction in power output and cycling performance. It is detected often because of an increase the internal resistance of the battery, leading to higher operating temperatures and reduced safety. In severe cases, separator clogging can lead to the formation of dendrites, which are small protrusions that can grow from one electrode to another, causing an internal short circuit and potentially leading to thermal runaway and battery failure.

To prevent separator clogging, battery designers and manufacturers employ various strategies such as selecting appropriate electrode materials, optimizing electrolyte composition, and using high-quality separators with appropriate pore sizes and porosity.

Battery users can also take precautions such as avoiding overcharging or overdischarging the battery, avoiding exposure to extreme temperatures, and using the battery within its specified operating conditions or SOA (Safe Operation Area).

Flame retardants: the key to keep safe redox running

To avoid uncontrolled redox reactions, flame-retardants are mixed in the cell construction and coating. The goal is to enhance the ignition resistance of lithium-ion battery components and to reduce the flammability of the electrolyte (often a very flammable and corrosive component).

Some of the most common flame retardants used in lithium-ion batteries are organic phosphate compounds, such as triphenylphosphate (TPP) and tributylphosphate (TBP). These additives can be mixed with the electrolyte solution at different concentrations (used of 0.5–2.0 wt% of TPP and TBP as flame retardants in a 1 M $LiPF_6$

/EC/DMC/DEC electrolyte solution or use of 2.5 wt% of encapsulated TPP and TBP as flame retardants in a 1 M $LiPF_6$ /EC/DMC electrolyte solution). TFP can also stand for bis(2,2,2-trifluoroethyl) ethylphosphonate (TFEP), which is a novel flame-retardant additive for conventional carbonate electrolyte that can enhance the thermal stability and ionic conductivity of lithium ion batteries. Hexamethylphosphoramide (HMPA) is also investigated as a flame retarding additive for lithium-ion batteries comprising solutions of $LiPF_6$ in organic carbonates. However, the HMPA causes a slight decrease in the conductivity (decreasing cycling performance) and narrower electrochemical stability window of the electrolyte.

Using a live cell

C-rate takes it all

Current load is of paramount relevance to design or choose a cell and will be further explained in the following volumes. Under a controlled environment (pressure, temperature, electric field), responding to an electrical load triggers up all mechanisms within the cell. Long before the ionic conductivity of the electrolyte has even been recalled, the very few ions in the surroundings of the membrane are ready to free some electrons to jump back towards the cathode. Once the jump through the separator is done, they repel other ions and are violently pushed to the bottom of the metal oxide crystals, generating an internal gradient of concentration initiating the chain reaction within the cell.

Such phenomena happen under all conditions, whether the cell is connected in series or parallel. The relevant metric is $Amps/m^2$, the specific current load, responsible of the underlying movements of ions within the cell and being time the secondary top metric. Hence, fast charging or high voltage charging of batteries do not change the main issue within the cell: its dynamic response in specific current terms.

C-rate is a measure of how fast a battery is charged or discharged relative to its capacity. The effect of C-rate on lithium battery cycle life depends on the type of battery and the temperature. In most cases, higher C-rates can reduce the cycle life of lithium batteries especially under low temperature conditions, due to the risk of lithium plating. However, some batteries can achieve better performance with localized high-concentration electrolytes (LHCE) that can prevent lithium plating.

Internal reactions absorb and release electrical, mechanical and thermal energy

One of the endothermic reactions in a lithium cell is the charging reaction, which absorbs heat from the surroundings. Another endothermic reaction is the conversion of some cathode materials such as $LiCoO_2$ or $LiMn_2O_4$ to lower oxidation states. These reactions increase the entropy of the system.

One of the exothermic reactions in a lithium cell is the discharging reaction, which releases heat to the surroundings. Another exothermic reaction is the decomposition of some anode materials such as lithiated graphite or SEI layer when exposed to electrolyte. These reactions increase the temperature and risk of thermal runaway. During charging, if they are overcharged or overheated, they can undergo exothermic reactions that release heat and cause thermal runaway. Some of these reactions include SEI layer decomposition, oxygen release from cathode, and electrolyte decomposition.

Temperature sensitivity

Temperature affects lithium battery cells during charge in different ways. Generally, lithium-ion cells can charge between 0°C and 60°C and can discharge between -20°C and 60°C. However, charging at high or low temperatures can reduce the cycle life or cause safety issues such as venting or plating. A standard operating temperature of 25±2°C during charge and discharge allows for the performance of the cell as per its datasheet.

Temperature varies the open circuit voltage (OCV) of a lithium cell by changing the thermodynamic potentials of the electrodes. Higher temperatures usually increase OCV, while lower temperatures decrease it. The temperature coefficient of voltage (TCV) is a measure of how much OCV changes with temperature.

Temperature affects lithium battery cells during discharge by changing their capacity too. Generally, higher temperatures increase the voltage and capacity of lithium battery cells, while lower temperatures decrease them. However, discharging at high temperatures can also reduce the cycle life or cause safety issues such as venting or fire.

Temperature affects the internal resistance of a lithium cell by changing the resistivity of the electrochemical materials and interfaces inside. Higher temperatures usually lower internal resistance, delivering higher power, while lower temperatures increase it. However, extreme temperatures (>50°C) can also damage or degrade lithium cells.

Lithium plating

Lithium plating is a side reaction where metallic lithium deposits on the negative electrode surface (anode during charging) by electrochemical reduction instead of intercalating into it. The phenomenon is especially notable at high currents, overcharging and/or low temperatures when there are no allocations to quickly place the ion flow. The overvoltage gives a thermodynamic advantage to the lithium aggregation over flowing forward due to the kinetic limitations and the inherent energy barrier for intercalation.

This reduces the capacity, performance and safety of lithium-ion batteries. It can be detected by various methods such as voltage measurements, impedance spectroscopy or post-mortem imaging techniques as:

1. Differential voltage analysis (DVA) can detect lithium plating by identifying a new peak induced by lithium plating on the differential voltage curve during discharging at low rates or rest. DVA can also quantify the amount of lithium plating by comparing the peak area with a pristine reference curve. Graphite anodes are designed with excess capacity over cathode to prevent plating.
2. Electrochemical impedance spectroscopy (EIS): EIS measures the battery's impedance as a function of frequency, and changes in impedance can indicate the presence of metallic lithium.
3. Direct observation: Techniques like scanning electron microscopy (SEM) or X-ray diffraction (XRD) can be used to directly observe lithium deposits on the anode surface.

Dendritic formation is a phenomenon that occurs when lithium metal grows in a tree-like structure on the anode of a lithium cell. This causes capacity loss and safety hazards if dendrites pierce the separator (short circuits), allowing free electron flow through.

Dendritic formation is caused by several factors, such as uneven current distribution, high current density, low temperature, poor electrolyte stability and low ion mobility.

To prevent dendritic formation, some strategies include using solid electrolytes, coating the anode with protective layers, adding additives to the electrolyte and optimizing the cell design. To date, all the mentioned mechanisms increase the cell internal impedance.

Mitigating or reversing lithium plating involves addressing its causes:

1. Charge rate: Charging the battery at a slower rate or using a tapered charging profile can help reduce lithium plating.
2. Design: designing the anode with excess capacity (10%) to host ions while maintaining an OCV voltage range within the electrolyte spec.
3. Temperature control: Maintaining the battery within an optimal temperature range can minimize the risk of lithium plating. Preheating the battery at low temperatures or using thermal management systems can help achieve this.
4. Battery design: Optimizing the anode material, surface morphology, and electrode structure can reduce the likelihood of lithium plating.
5. Electrolyte additives: Some additives can enhance the stability of the SEI layer upon formation, improving lithium-ion intercalation and reducing the propensity for lithium plating.
6. External voltage control: Applying an external voltage to reverse the lithium plating process, although this can be challenging to implement and control.

By understanding the causes of lithium plating and employing mitigation strategies, it's possible to extend the life and safety of lithium-ion batteries.

Lithium stripping is the process of removing lithium metal from the anode surface by electrochemical oxidation. It is the reverse reaction of lithium plating, Lithium stripping and plating are side reactions that occur during the discharging and charging of lithium-ion batteries, and in no case are selective, so forced lithium oxidation will induce or trigger other undesired side reactions in parallel.

Battery venting

Battery venting is a phenomenon where a battery releases hot gas due to internal pressure build-up. Battery venting can be caused by various factors such as puncturing, overcharging, manufacturing defect or thermal runaway by gas evolution due to chemical reactions inside the cell. It damages the battery and poses safety risks as hot gases are channeled by the collector plates towards the cell walls.

One established countermeasure that is built-in within a cell to limit gas build-up and to facilitate cell venting is a pressure burst disk or purposely weakened seal that opens (breaks) when the cell's internal pressure exceeds a critical value. This can prevent the cell from explosive rupturing due to excessive gas generation. In lab designs, venting is prevented by embedding sensor technology in small cells that can monitor the cell venting byproducts formation, such as hydrogen, oxygen and carbon dioxide, and alert the user or trigger a safety mechanism to prevent full thermal runaway and, if so, small amounts of energy can be released.

A long-lasting life: cyclability

Cycle life of a lithium cell is being modeled by various methods that consider different factors affecting battery degradation. Some common factors are temperature, depth of discharge, discharge rate, end of charge voltage, film resistance, and parasitic reactions. Some models use machine learning algorithms to predict remaining useful life based on charge/discharge data.

There are different models that can be used to model cycle life aging of lithium cells, depending on the type of aging mechanism and parameter. The most studied types of aging mechanisms are calendar aging and cycling aging.

Calendar aging is a type of aging process that leads to a degradation of a lithium cell independent of charge-discharge cycling, with no load current applied. It is mainly caused by losses of lithium ions to the solid-electrolyte interphase (SEI) layer on the electrodes. Calendar aging is affected by factors such as temperature, state of charge and storage duration. Some experiments may force the cell to be stored at constant voltage instead, often around or above the highest State of Charge (SoC).

Calendar aging can be measured by monitoring changes in capacity and impedance of a lithium cell over time under different storage conditions as temperature, pressure and voltage.

An always ready cell is a risk

Generally, holding lithium batteries at full voltage can reduce their cycle life and capacity due to side reactions and degradation of the electrodes. However, some lithium batteries, such as lithium iron phosphate (LFP), can tolerate higher voltages beyond nominal without significant damage.

Side reactions are unwanted chemical reactions that occur in lithium batteries during charging or discharging. They can consume the active materials, degrade the electrolyte, form deposits on the electrodes, generate heat and gas, and reduce the performance and safety of the battery. Some examples of side reactions are lithium plating, carbon corrosion, electrolyte oxidation and reduction, collector corrosion, shuttle effect of redox mediators and contamination by air.

There are different ways to suppress side reactions in lithium batteries, depending on the type of reaction and the battery chemistry. Some common methods are:

- Using electrolytes that are stable at high voltages and compatible with both electrodes.
- Coating the electrodes with protective layers that prevent direct contact with the electrolyte.
- Adding additives or redox mediators to the electrolyte that can scavenge reactive species or facilitate charge transfer.
- Optimizing the cell design and operating conditions to avoid overcharging, overheating and lithium plating.

Redox mediators are chemicals that can transfer electrons between different substances. They can help speed up electrochemical reactions by shuttling electrons between the electrode and the reactants. In context, some redox mediators can improve the efficiency of batteries or fuel cells by reducing the overpotential.

Overpotential is the difference between the actual voltage and the theoretical voltage of a battery, and it reduces the efficiency and performance of a battery. It represents the extra energy needed to overcome various resistances in the battery, such as charge transfer, mass transport, and ohmic losses. It is normally seen in voltammograms as hysteresis.

Different types of overpotential may require different strategies to reduce them. For example, ohmic overpotential can be reduced by using conductive materials and minimizing the distance between electrodes, while activation overpotential can be reduced by using efficient catalysts and increasing the reaction surface area.

Capacity fade, power decrease and voltage drop: inefficiency

The main causes of lithium cells capacity fade are the loss of lithium inventory (LLI) and the loss of active material (LAM). LLI is caused by side reactions between the electrodes and the electrolyte, which consume lithium ions and reduce the available charge carriers. LAM is caused by structural degradation of the electrodes, which reduces their ability to store and release lithium ions. Both LLI and LAM are influenced by various factors such as temperature, current rate, state of charge, and cycling history.

There are different stages and mechanisms of capacity fade in lithium cells depending on the operating conditions and cycling history. Some of the common side reactions that cause LLI are the formation of a SEI layer on the anode surface, which consumes lithium ions and electrolyte solvents, and the dissolution of transition metal ions from the cathode into the electrolyte, which reduces the active material and increases impedance. Some of the common factors that cause LAM are mechanical stress, volume change, phase transition, and particle cracking in the electrodes (inducing larger SEI formation). These factors affect both electrodes but are more pronounced in the anode.

Power decrease in lithium-ion batteries is a result of various ageing mechanisms that affect the capacity and performance of the cells. Some of these mechanisms include:

- Reaction of active materials with electrolyte at electrodes interfaces
- Self-degradation of active materials structure on cycling
- Aging of non-active components

Reaction of active materials with electrolyte is one of the ageing mechanisms that causes power decrease in lithium-ion batteries. This process involves the decomposition of the electrolyte (the liquid or solid substance that allows ions to move between electrodes) due to thermal stress, cell operation conditions, or chemical reactions with the electrodes.

Self-degradation of active materials structure is another ageing mechanism that causes power decrease in lithium-ion batteries. This process involves the physical and chemical changes that occur within the electrodes during charge and discharge cycles. Some of these changes include:

- Phase transitions that can cause volume expansion and contraction, cracking, and loss of contact among active, conductive surfaces, causing insulation
- Dissolution of transition metals from cathode materials into electrolyte
- Plating of metallic lithium on anode surface
- Loss of active lithium inventory due to side reactions

Side reactions do not only take place between cell active materials but also with any other material available within the cell envelope. Traces of dust, water, adhesives, lube and metal traces from handling, are prone to launch side reactions and generate undesired by-products which may remain in suspension or releasing gas inavertently.

Charge: risk in the short run

A lithium cell should be mainly charged using a constant-current/constant-voltage (CC/CV) charging step. This means that the cell is charged with a constant current until it reaches a certain voltage, then the current is reduced to maintain a fixed voltage until the cell is fully charged. Staggered charges, refresh charges and pulses are also used along the process.

The charging temperature should be around 25°C for optimal performance and safety of most chemistries and differs for each one. Charging outside the recommended cell envelope may damage the cell or reduce its lifespan. However, special charge cycles after cold-start may reach higher temperatures at the end of charge to relax plating formation.

Overcharge is a dangerous condition for a lithium cell that can cause irreversible damage or even trigger a fire, rapid disassembly or explosion. Overcharge occurs when the cell voltage exceeds its upper limit due to excessive current or faulty charging control.

Damage occur due to chemical reactions inside the cell that degrade its components, such as electrolyte, electrodes, and separator. It can also cause lithium dendrites to form on the surface of the battery anode, which can create short circuits inside the battery. These effects can result in over-pressurization, high temperature, and thermal runaway of the cell.

During charging, some overpotential is required to insert the lithium ions in the graphite interlayer. This overpotential is reduced with temperature allowing faster and less damaging charges at the expense of electrode expansion and pressure build-up.

Discharge: risks in the long run

For reference purposes, a lithium cell should be discharged with a constant current until it reaches a cut-off voltage that is determined by the cell chemistry and design. Discharging below this voltage may damage the cell or reduce its capacity.

The discharging temperature should mostly be within -20°C and 60°C for optimal performance and safety. Discharging outside this range may affect the cell performance, voltage or internal resistance.

When underdischarged, lithium-ion batteries can develop dendrites which are needle-like structures that grow from the anode and can cause short circuits and electrode corrosion which may ultimately cause separator clog. Sustained undervoltage can also increase the internal resistance of the battery, which reduces its voltage output and causes heat generation.

Lithium anode dissolution is the process of electrochemical oxidation of lithium surface atoms that release cations into the electrolyte. This happens during stripping in lithium metal batteries. The diffusion and migration of lithium cations across the SEI have been determined to be the main contributors to the stripping overpotential. Two modes of stripping are being studied based on the passivation condition of lithium: stripping on passivated lithium and pitting on lithium after SEI layer breakdown.

Lithium cathode can also be dissolved during operation. This happens when transition metal ions from the cathode material dissolve into the electrolyte due to newly-formed acidic species such as hydrogen fluoride. The dissolution of transition metal ions is influenced by factors such as undesired species in the electrolyte, temperature, voltage and cycling conditions, degrading battery performance.

A separator clog occurs when the pores of the separator are blocked by impurities or deposits from the electrodes or electrolyte. This effectively reduces the ion transport capability and increase the internal resistance of the battery.

Made in the USA
Columbia, SC
06 November 2023